Now What?

Now What?

Santiego Rivers

Now What?

Copyright © 2021 by **Santiego Rivers**

All rights reserved. This book may not be reproduced or transmitted in any form without the written permission of the author.

Now What?

If you are not willing to learn, no one can help you.

If you are determined to learn, no one can stop you

- Unknown

Now What?

In this book, you will find questions that could lead to the answers that will inspire you to ask questions that could change your life.

(I say again) In this book, you will find questions that could lead to the answers that will inspire you to ask questions that could change your life.

This book will reveal and explain the graduation requirements for High Schools in the State of Florida. This book will also break-down how graduating from High School is not enough to prepare many scholars for their future.

I wrote this book because it was in my heart to speak knowledge and wisdom to those who need to know that someone cares about their future and is willing to make their voice heard.

I wrote this book for many scholars to learn that graduation is the starting line and not the finishing line for their future.

Life begins after graduation, which is why you must plan your life before you graduate.

Now What?

- My high school years **(6-9)**
- Skills & knowledge that many scholars lack even after graduation **(10-12)**
- Facing our fears **(13)**
- Life after graduation **(14-15)**
- What are the graduation requirements in the State of Florida? **(16-17)**
- What is a Certificate of Completion? **(18)**
- What is a Special Diploma? **(19)**
- What is the purpose of graduation? **(20-21)**
- Flaws in the system **(22-23)**
- The powers that be **(24-25)**
- How are you investing in your future? **(26)**
- Year-by-Year Checklist **(27-30)**
- What is your next step? **(31-32)**

My high school years

I often reminisce about my high school years leading up to my graduation; many moons ago. I often wonder how different my life could have been if I had made a few other choices in my life before graduation.

I often wonder if I learned more while I was in school or when I entered the real world after graduation?

What I do know is that my high school years went by fast. I remember walking the hallways as a scared and nervous freshman, becoming a senior holding onto those same uncomfortable feelings for a whole different reason. I didn't feel like I was ready to face the real world.

As a freshman in high school, I felt like a little fish leaving his pond entering a river. The year prior, I was the big fish in a small pond, but now, things have changed.

Everything about high school seemed different than what I was used to in middle school. The campus was bigger than I was used to coming

Now What?

from middle school. The other scholars seemed like adults compared to me in high school.

I was fortunate to have neighborhood friends and family members attending the same school with me, but deep inside, I was still afraid of the new environment.

Eventually, I was able to adjust to my new environment and the people around me. I admit that there were a lot of growing pains along the way for me in High School.

Having plenty of friends and family members attending the same school helped me a lot when it came to me adjusting to my new environment.

Being a student-athlete helped me feel more comfortable at school, but I knew that I would be leaving school very soon.

Even though I would be the first person to graduate from high school in my family and even attend college, graduating high school left me feeling empty inside.

While most of my peers danced across the stage during the graduation ceremony, I managed to put on a smile for my mother and family members in attendance as I walked off the stage.

Now What?

I couldn't understand how many of my peers could dance across the stage, knowing that they would be reporting to a minimum wage job within a few hours while still living with their parents after graduating.

I didn't understand why I was walking the stage with peers that I knew were dumber than a box of rocks, but they were graduating.

I fully understood that if you wanted to know which students are most likely to be the scholars who have special diplomas or really shouldn't be graduating, the ways to discover it was simple.

Take the time to attend a graduation ceremony and watch them dance across the stage for their last fifteen minutes of fame. Therefore, I always say, *"Let the clowns have the circus."*

Now What?

After graduation, it would take me years to learn that school did not adequately prepare me for the real world.

I take full responsibility for my part of not being prepared for life after school, but as an aware adult, I realize the many flaws within our school system that fails its students.

The main problem that I dislike about the school system was the business part of schools over the school's real purpose. The school's real goal is for the betterment of the scholars who attended.

Scholars attend school to gain the skills and education needed to live freely and successfully in the real world. School also teaches scholars the skills they will need in their future lives and careers.

How can you remove many vocational training courses in school and expect scholars to be ready to enter the workforce to live freely and successfully after graduation?

Many schools are graded and judged on their scholars' test scores, which does not calculate scholars' real strengths and their ability to live freely and successfully in their lives.

Skills & knowledge that many scholars lack even after graduation

There are many skills and essential things that many scholars still lack even after graduation.

What are some of the skills graduates' lack?

- Writing proficiency. ...
- Public speaking. ...
- Data analysis. ...
- Critical thinking/problem-solving. ...
- Attention to detail. ...
- Communication. ...
- Leadership. ...
- Teamwork.

These are a few of the needed skills that tests cannot accurately access in scholars, which leads to my next question. How will scholars improve their needed skills?

1. Find out what they are good at
2. Learn to work in their learning style to show their strengths.
3. Be involved in activities that will require them to use their strengths.
4. Enroll in courses and electives that can enhance them.

Now What?

5. Keep using their skills while learning to develop others.
6. Practice, practice, and practice.
7. Watch online video tutorials and not just be lectured all day.
8. Learn from the experts where they can teach their scholars.
9. Do not be content with your current level. You must apply yourself
10. Monitor your growth. Create a vision board and a portfolio of your success
11. Give time and focus through consistency. Don't become discouraged.

The responsibility falls on the shoulders of the scholars, teachers, principals, and the people who witness this travesty occurring each day to say and do something to make the powers to change the system that governs our schools.

Here are a few of the things that scholars need to know about life after graduation and how they can discover the ability to become successful in life.

Now What?

- Not everyone needs to go to college to be successful in life.
- Only you can determine how far and how high you will go in life.
- Discover your potential and develop your craft.
- You must learn to apply yourself to your craft.
- Be completely transparent.
- Always be willing to learn.
- Create value within yourself that others will need.
- Your network is vital to your success in life
- Study the habits of successful people.
- Mirror the habits of people who found success in the area you want to master.
- Never operate from a position of fear.

Fear stops many people from acting when action is needed.

Facing our Fears

We must learn to become fighters. We must learn to fight for the things that we want out of life because no one will give us anything.

In the game of life, there will be winners, and there must be losers. Only you can determine which fate will be yours? How bad do you want success?

Facing my fears is one skill or ability that I wished I learned or developed in school before graduation. I don't remember teachers or counselors in high school working with me to see where my strengths were and my plans after graduation.

It does not help to have parents or guardians who did not graduate high school to help you find your purpose in life. My mom struggled to keep food on the table and the bills paid. What about your parents or guardians?

Not having someone to turn to and guide you in the right direction makes facing life after graduation a scary thing. Yes, I was going to college on both an academic and athletic scholarship, but I knew inside that I did not want to play sports, and I was unsure what I wanted to do with my life after graduation.

Life after graduation

The people around you expect you to have your whole life after graduation figured out. The problem with that opinion is that your mindset is still that of a child inside an adult body.

A few scholars are ready for graduation after high school, but most scholars are big fish swimming in a river going to the real world, which is an ocean after graduation.

In my opinion, if your career path does not require you to have a college degree, investigate going to a vocational/ trade school or even the military after graduation. Continue your education. Never stop learning.

One of the best things about going to **college** is the ability to continue your education and experience college life, including its many traditions and organizations.

Many high-paying jobs require college credit hours, including a college degree. The whole college experience is a once-in-a-lifetime opportunity.

One of the best things about going to a **vocational / trade school** is that it is cheaper than most colleges, and you spend your time focusing on the skills you will need for your trade. Basically, you get to making money faster than if you went to college.

One of the best things about going to the **military** is its benefits and the opportunity to serve our country. My wife served 20 years in the Navy; now, she is retired with honors and going to school for free, while I am still working full time and paying off student loans. We are close to the same age!

One of the best things about going into the workforce after graduation is the ability to start earning money right away and establish your independence.

You must determine what the best path for you to take after graduation is. Don't wait until your senior year to get serious about your future. Talk with someone and explore the different options.

Don't settle for the option; that is the easiest thing to do. Pick an option that will require you to work hard, not have to struggle, and live paycheck to paycheck for the rest of your life.

Do you even know the graduation requirements it will take to start your future?

Now What?

What are the graduation requirements in the State of Florida?

For scholars to graduate in the State of Florida with a regular **24 Credit** High School Diploma, scholars are required to complete the following criteria:

- 4 years of English
- 4 years of math that must include Algebra and Geometry
- 3 years of science that must include:
1. Biology
2. U.S. History
3. World History
4. American Government
5. Economics

- HOPE (2 semesters)
- 1 online course
- Pass Algebra EOC and FSA ELA (or concordant) or waiver
- Must reach 24 credits
- GPA over 2.0 (round up from 1.95)

Now What?

For scholars to graduate in the State of Florida with an **18 Credit** High School Diploma, scholars are required to complete the following criteria:

For 18:
Same as 24 except no Hope or online course requirement, only need 18 credits.
- 4 years of English
- 4 years of math that must include Algebra and Geometry
- 3 years of science that must include:
6. Biology
7. U.S. History
8. World History
9. American Government
10. Economics

- Pass Algebra EOC and FSA ELA (or concordant) or waiver
- Must reach 24 credits
- GPA over 2.0 (round up from 1.95)

For a certificate of completion **(non-grad):** Scholars who have met all other requirements have not passed a reading or math test, including a GPA below 2.0. A COC is not a graduate and is not eligible for Federal Financial Aid.

What is a Special Diploma?

A special Diploma is an option that Florida and the school districts offer to students with disabilities who cannot meet the requirements for a **Standard Diploma**.

It must be understood that a **Special Diploma** does not have meaning in the job market or for post-secondary educational opportunities.

In 2014, two options for students with disabilities to obtain a standard diploma occurred.

The Standard Diploma via Access Points and ***The Standard Diploma Option for Students with Disabilities Pathway***.

The Standard Diploma via Access Points offers an academic option to the Standard Diploma for students with disabilities. This option includes those with more significant intellectual and developmental disabilities. It provided a modified curriculum.

The Standard Diploma Option for Students with Disabilities Pathway provided students with the most significant intellectual and developmental disabilities an employment competency pathway.

Now What?

What is a Certificate of Completion?

Students who cannot achieve a **Standard Diploma** in the State of Florida will receive a **Certificate of Completion**. As mentioned earlier, there are more requirements involved in a scholar obtaining a **Standard Diploma**.

The **Certificate of Completion** is a certificate of *attendance and record coursework completed* while attending High School.

The 2014 legislation requires parents to declare their students' intention to pursue either a **Standard Diploma or a Certificate of Completion.** Parents had to decide as to the best path to take for their children.

The Certificate of Completion is not a goal scholar would work towards in school. It is more of a way of allowing scholars to feel a sense of accomplishment.

Presenting the certificate of completion as an option of choice could result in many students who do not earn any diploma in the end.

What is the purpose of graduation?

Traditionally, Graduation Ceremonies Celebrate Student Achievements. The purpose of a high school graduation ceremony is to celebrate students who have successfully met the **academic and extracurricular requirements** for graduation.

The statement does not mention anything about a student being ready to deal with life after school. The **academic and extracurricular requirements** for graduation do not give the student the essential skills they will need in life.

You have many scholars graduating from schools who do not read, write, or comprehend beyond a middle school grade level and sometimes even lower.

These same scholars do not even possess the life skills to balance a checkbook or understand how working at a fast-food restaurant will never allow them to move out of their parents' house for years.

I have witnessed this on many different levels. As a student, a graduate, a Teacher Aide, Teacher & Behavior Specialist.

Now What?

Many counties, especially in Florida, brag about their graduation rates but fail to explain why their numbers are high.

One county in Florida bragged about having a record-high graduation rate for the 2018-2019 school year while failing to mention that many of these graduates were sacrificial lambs to the system.

As a Certified Teacher and employee in a Florida school district, I have witnessed how the current policies are put in place to help the schools more than help the overall students' success.

The following is a prime example of how the current policy works in my district.

A student who does not apply themselves in their academic course most of the time; the lowest grade that the teacher can give them is approximately 50%.

This current system allows the student the chance to finish the class with a "D" or even higher if they turn in any work before the end of the grading period.

Many students quickly learn how the system works and takes full advantage of its flaws.

Now What?

Flaws in the system

There are many flaws that we can point out when it comes to the Educational System. Deficiencies in the Educational System range from the following, but is not limited to:

- **Parents are not involved enough**
- **Our schools are overcrowded.**
- **Technology comes with its downsides.**
- **School spending is stagnant, even in our improving economy.**
- **We are still using the teacher training methods of yesterday.**
- **There is a lack of teacher education innovation**
- **Some students are lost to the school-to-prison pipeline.**
- **We still do not know how to handle high school dropouts.**
- **We have not achieved education equity**
- **We still struggle with making teacher tenure benefit both students and teachers.**
- **More of our schools need to consider year-round schooling.**
- **We are still wrestling with the achievement gap**

Now What?

- **We need to consider how school security measures affect students**
- **We need to make assistive technology more available for students with disabilities.**

Each of these flaws/deficiencies deserves their book related to how they negatively affect scholars.

I want to shed light on the removal of needed courses that could have greatly help our scholars in the real world.

Courses like **Home Economics** and **Auto shop** have been removed out of many schools.

Home Economics and **Shop** class were offered to middle and high school scholars as electives. These classes allowed scholars to get prepared for their lives as adults after graduation.

If you wonder how the removal of these elective classes could happen, the answer is simple.

The people responsible for making decisions about schools' needs and the students that their choices affect do not have any educational background.

Now What?

The Powers that be

Before we talk about the people who decide about our local schools' issues, we must first look at how our schools are funded.

School funding comes from a variety of federal, state, and city money pots. Approximately 46 percent of public spending on elementary and secondary schools comes from local government budgets.

One reason for the large disparity in spending is the size of the local tax base. To provide students with more significant elective opportunities, each school community must have local financial support.

There is some money allocated nationally for schools. The individual local taxpayers distribute a large portion of the funds available for schools.

You may have to reread this section to understand that our schools are dependent upon people to allocate money to our schools and programs that don't care about public education.

Their kids attend private schools. Need I say anything more?

Now What?

Having a person with no background in education make important decisions about education is like having a President of the United States of America with no political experience running our country.

Let us view the requirements for School Board Candidates. While the following may be standard criteria necessary to run for school board, it does vary by state and district. A school board candidate may be asked to meet the following requirements:

1. Be a registered voter.
2. Be a resident of the district that the individual is running to represent.
3. At least have a high school diploma or a certificate of equivalency.
4. Not a convicted felon.
5. Not be a current employee of the district or be related to a current employee in that district.

Hopefully, you noticed that having a background in education or even Business Management is not a requirement to control decisions that affect a generation of scholars.

How are you investing in your future?

Now What?

High school is an exciting and often stressful time for many scholars. Transitioning from middle school to high school is a significant cultural shark.

Scholars must know there are useful tools and resources available to help them prepare for their future. Hopefully, this book helps them learn what to do to start investing in their future.

Scholars need to learn how to map out a plan with a year-by-year checklist. This checklist is a vision board that includes keeping track of everything you have accomplished, including the things you still need to do.

The following is a year-by-year checklist of the basic things you need to start working on to prepare you for your future.

Now What?

Freshman Year

First-year students should take every opportunity to make themselves stand out among their peers. Here are some of the steps they can take:

1. **Create a yearly schedule for achieving graduation requirements.** School guidance counselors can help students develop a plan.
2. **Explore career interests by conducting online research and attending career fairs.** *Prep STEP* offers career factsheets, articles, and e-books that help students make informed decisions about securing a job in their desired field.
3. **Begin participating in leadership or community-based activities.** Many high schools require **community service hours** for graduation. Students should continue involvement in these activities throughout high school.
4. **Sharpen core academic skills.** Develop your English language arts, social studies, biology, chemistry, earth science, physics, math, and computers.
5. **Cultivate good study habits.**

Now What?

Sophomore Year

Learning how to manage school and extracurricular activities can be challenging enough without factoring in college or career exploration. Sophomores should schedule a time for these activities:

1. **Take more challenging classes.** Many high schools offer honors and AP-level courses in core academic subjects and rigorous career and technical education classes.
2. **Build workplace skills.** Even part-time jobs require students to demonstrate professional behavior.
3. **Attend college and career fairs.**
4. **Reach out to mentors in fields of interest.** Ask questions about their careers and arrange to shadow them for a day.
5. **Prepare for the PSAT/NMSQT®.**

Junior Year

Junior year is an important year for students, especially if they are college-bound. It's the year students begin taking college admissions exams. Here is a list of what they should do:

1. **Take the PSAT/ NMSQT®.** Students must take the test by grade 11 to qualify for the **National Merit Scholarship Program**.
2. **Schedule campus visits.** It's essential to select a college or university that is the right fit. **Campus visits** offer a glimpse into what life there would be like and help students narrow their choices.
3. **Research ways to pay for college.** Options include scholarships, student loans, and **federal student aid** for eligible applicants. *Prep Step*'s Scholarship Finder enables students to search for more than 24,000 scholarships and other awards.
4. **Take the SAT and ACT.**
5. **Request transcripts and letters of recommendation** from teachers and mentors.

Now What?

Senior Year

By senior year, most students should have clearly defined goals. Here are some key activities to focus on:

1. **Take (or retake) college admissions or career certification exams.**
2. **Complete and submit college applications.** Find an excellent source to guide you on how to write your college admissions essays.
3. **Complete and submit scholarship applications.**
4. **Keep grades up and verify that all your graduation requirements will be met on schedule.** Students and their guidance counselors should be keeping track.
5. **Optional: Take an AP® exam.** Offered each May, AP exams provide students an opportunity to demonstrate mastery of college-level material and earn college credit at most colleges and universities in the U.S. and Canada.

Now What?

What is your next step?

Life begins after graduation, which is why you must plan your life before you graduate. Graduation is the starting line, not the finish line.

Are you afraid to run your race? It would help if you learned to fear not fulfilling your dreams and goals.

Fear kills dreams, but preparation helps them come true. What are you doing to make your dreams come true?

After receiving all this information regarding preparing for your future after graduation, what will you do with it?

You must learn how to make your next move your best move when it comes to your future. After reading this book, the only person left to blame if you end up with a future less than you desire is yourself.

You are the master of your universe. Your parents, your teachers, or your friends can't turn your dreams into reality.

Now What?

No one can make you want what you don't want for yourself. You must want it and desire it to make it possible. What do you want? Are you willing to work hard for it?

If the answer is yes:

Learn to say less and start doing more in your life. Learn to get in touch with your greatness. Make your life make sense to you and no one else.

You must be willing to get comfortable with being uncomfortable as you make the needed changes in your life.

The time is now to act. Once you reached high school, the sand in the hourglass began to fall. Where will you be when the sand in the hourglass has all fallen? Will you be ready for the beginning of your life as an adult?

Even if this book did not give you all the answers you need, it gave you a guide to the things you will need to do to accomplish your dreams.

Are you ready Dream Chaser???

Now What?

Notes

Now What?

Notes

Now What?

Notes

References

Bhuiya, C. (2017, May 2). *The Skills Gap is Real: 8 Skills You Didn't Know You Needed.* GoSkills.Com. https://www.goskills.com/Soft-Skills/Resources/Skills-gap

Preparing for Life After High School: A Four-Year Checklist for Students. (n.d.). Https://Www.Ebsco.Com/. Retrieved January 17, 2021, from https://www.ebsco.com/blogs/ebscopost/preparing-life-after-high-school-four-year-checklist-students

www.ingramcontent.com/pod-product-compliance
Lightning Source LLC
Chambersburg PA
CBHW071339190426
43193CB00042B/2042